STECK

COMPREHENSION SKILLS

INFERENCE

LEVEL C

STECK-VAUGHN
ELEMENTARY · SECONDARY · ADULT · LIBRARY

A Harcourt Company

www.steck-vaughn.com

Editorial Director:	Diane Schnell
Project Editor:	Anne Souby
Associate Director of Design:	Cynthia Ellis
Design Manager:	Cynthia Hannon
Media Researcher:	Christina Berry
Production:	Karen Wilburn
Cover Illustration:	Stephanie Carter
Cover Production:	Alan Klemp
Photograph:	©CORBIS

ISBN 0-7398-2639-5

Making an inference means making a guess. You can make this guess by putting together what you know and what you read or see. You will make inferences about the stories in this book.

You make inferences all the time. Look at the picture. Have you ever planted a garden? How do you think the person in this picture feels? What helped you make this inference?

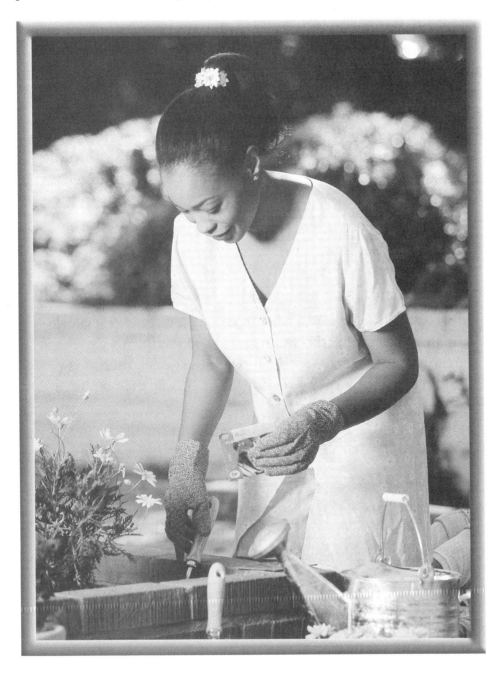

What Is an Inference?

An inference is a guess you make after thinking about what you already know. Suppose a friend invites you to a picnic. From what you know about picnics, you might infer that there will be food and drinks, and you will eat outside.

An author does not write every detail in a story. If every detail were told, a story would be long and boring. And the main point would be lost. Suppose you read, "Lynn went to a restaurant." The writer does not have to tell you what a restaurant is. You already know that it is a place where people go to eat a meal. From what you know, you might imagine that Lynn looked at a menu. Then a server took her order. By filling in these missing details, you could infer that Lynn went to the restaurant to eat. You can infer this by putting together what you read and what you already know.

Try It!

Read this story. Think about the facts in the story.

◆

> Earthquakes can cause a lot of damage. This is especially true in places where the soil is loose and damp. An earthquake can turn loose, damp soil into thick mud. Buildings will sink or fall down. Many people may be hurt.

What can you infer? Write an inference on the line below.

_____

You might have written something such as "An earthquake can harm a city." You can make this inference from what the story tells you about earthquakes and what you already know.

Practice Making Inferences

In units 1 through 12 of this book, you will be asked to answer the question "Which of these sentences is probably true?" Read the following story.

Red-crowned cranes are beautiful birds. They are known for their trumpeting call. Many of these cranes live on an island in Japan. They live in marshes and are protected by law. But there are fewer than two thousand cranes left. They are in danger of disappearing.

___B___ **1.** Which of these sentences is probably true?
>   **A.** The Japanese don't care about these cranes.
>   **B.** People in Japan want to help the cranes.
>   **C.** Red-crowned cranes live in the desert.
>   **D.** There are too many cranes in Japan.

Only one answer is a good choice. Read answer **B**. It is the best choice. The story says that these cranes are in danger of disappearing and that they are protected by law. From the story you can infer that people in Japan want to help these cranes.

Read the following story. Answer it on your own.

Ted was a baby and knew only a few words. One day he pointed to a dog and said, "Dog!" His mother praised him for learning a new word. The next day Ted pointed to a cat and said, "Dog!" Later a squirrel ran by. Ted pointed and shouted, "Dog!"

_____ **2.** Which of these sentences is probably true?
>   **A.** Ted wanted his bottle.
>   **B.** Ted was afraid of dogs.
>   **C.** Ted thought all small animals were called dogs.
>   **D.** Ted liked cats better than squirrels.

To check your answer, turn to page 60.

More Practice Making Inferences

In units 13 through 25 of this book, you will do a new kind of exercise. Each story is followed by statements. Some of the statements are inferences. Others are facts. Decide whether each statement is an inference or a fact. Read this story.

> Ben moved from England to Maine. In England he was taught to stand up when answering a question. So in his new class, he stood up when the teacher called on him. Some of the other students laughed at him. After class the teacher told him that he could stay in his seat when she called on him.

Fact	Inference		
○	●	**1. A.**	Ben was a polite person.
●	○	**B.**	Ben moved from England to Maine.
○	●	**C.**	The teacher wanted to help Ben.
●	○	**D.**	Some students laughed at Ben.

You can find statements **B** and **D** in the story. So they are facts. We can infer from the way he acts that Ben is a polite person. But this isn't stated in the story. So **A** is an inference. We can guess from the teacher's actions that she wanted to help Ben. So **C** is also an inference.

Read this story. Mark your answers.

> Pigs are smart. They can learn many tricks. They can fetch sticks, dance, and tumble. It takes a pig less time than a dog to learn tricks. Pigs like people and are very curious. Pigs can even learn to open gates and locks.

Fact	Inference		
○	○	**2. A.**	Pigs can learn to open locks.
○	○	**B.**	Pigs can learn many tricks.
○	○	**C.**	Pigs are smarter than dogs.
○	○	**D.**	Pigs are curious.

To check your answers, turn to page 60.

How to Use This Book

Read the stories in this book. Answer the question across the page from each story. You can check your answers yourself. If you wish, tear out pages 61 and 62. Find the unit you want to check. Fold the answer page on the dotted line to show the correct unit. Write the number of correct answers in the score box at the top of the page.

Remember

In this book there are two kinds of multiple-choice exercises. In units 1 through 12, you are asked, "Which of these sentences is probably true?" From what you read and what you know, you can choose the best answer. In units 13 through 25, you are asked to decide whether each statement is a fact or an inference.

Hints for Better Reading

- As you read, keep in mind the difference between facts and inferences.
- Think about the facts in the story. Think about what you already know. Make an inference by putting together what you know and what you've read.

Challenge Yourself

Read each story. Write one more inference you can make about each story.

Writing

On pages 30–31 and 58–59, there are stories with questions. These do not have answers for you to choose. Think of an answer. Write it in your own words. You will find suggested answers on page 60. But your answers may be different.

1. Joe was a teen-age chess player. He thought he was a pretty good player. So he decided to play more than a hundred people at once. Just twenty people showed up to play him, though. And eighteen of those beat him, including a small boy.

2. It was 1865. A train moved slowly from town to town. It was going from Washington, D.C., to Illinois. The body of Abraham Lincoln was on the train. People stood on both sides of the tracks in each town. They stood quietly as the train passed. Their eyes were full of tears.

3. John loved to fish. He went fishing anytime he could. The weather was very hot and dry. John sat on the shore, thinking about catching fish. But the fish just would not bite. All day John waited patiently. He was hungry and thirsty. But even as the sun went down, he did not move.

4. The dog hurried home. It had a juicy bone in its mouth. It could hardly wait to get home to enjoy its meal. As the dog crossed a stream, it stopped in the middle of the bridge. It looked in the still water. There it saw another dog with a bone in its mouth. The dog thought it could bark and scare away the other dog. Then it could have that bone, too. But as the dog barked, its bone fell in the water. Then the other dog disappeared.

5. In 1659 the country of Sweden made some new money. These metal coins were quite large. And they were hard to use. Each one weighed more than thirty pounds. They were the largest coins in history.

_____ **1.** Which of these sentences is probably true?
      A. Joe wasn't a good chess player.
      B. Some of Joe's chess pieces were lost.
      C. Joe didn't try to win because he was tired.
      D. The other players were sick and couldn't come.

_____ **2.** Which of these sentences is probably true?
      A. The people did not like trains.
      B. The train didn't make very much noise.
      C. The people were sad that Lincoln had died.
      D. The train had never been to Illinois before.

_____ **3.** Which of these sentences is probably true?
      A. There were no fish in the water.
      B. John wanted to stay until he caught a fish.
      C. Other people were fishing at the pond.
      D. John went home early for dinner.

_____ **4.** Which of these sentences is probably true?
      A. The dog wasn't hungry.
      B. It was a rainy day.
      C. The bone was not heavy.
      D. The dog was greedy.

_____ **5.** Which of these sentences is probably true?
      A. The coins were not very pretty.
      B. The Swedish people stopped using the coins.
      C. Other countries started making large coins, too.
      D. The Swedish people did not like history.

1. The village people chose a boy to guard the sheep. It was an important job. If a wolf came near, the boy was supposed to call the people in the village. Then they would come to help him. The boy watched the sheep for a little while. Then he decided to have some fun. He cried out loudly, "Wolf! Wolf!" The people rushed out to fight the wolf. When they arrived the boy was laughing at them. There was no wolf.

2. Huck Finn had a friend named Jim, but Jim was a slave. Jim was always sad, and he didn't smile very often. Huck decided to help Jim escape to freedom.

3. Jan Ernst Matzeliger worked in a shoe factory. In the 1800s, making shoes was slow. Shoes were made by hand. Each person could make only a few pairs a day. Matzeliger liked machines. He made a machine that could make several hundred pairs of shoes a day. This meant that everyone could afford shoes.

4. Clara Barton was a nurse. She treated soldiers during the Civil War. After the war, she went to Europe to work for the Red Cross. She helped people in trouble. Barton returned to the United States. She wanted to start a Red Cross in America. Many people gave her money. She started the American Red Cross in 1881. She was in charge of it for 23 years.

5. You have probably seen a rainbow in the sky. What does it take to form a rainbow? There are three conditions for a rainbow to form. First, there must be many raindrops in the sky. Second, the sun must be shining on the raindrops. Third, the sun must be behind you. Then the rainbow will be in front of you.

_____ **1.** Which of these sentences is probably true?
    A. Everyone thought the joke was funny.
    B. Several of the sheep got lost.
    C. The people were angry at the boy.
    D. The boy was very kind.

_____ **2.** Which of these sentences is probably true?
    A. Jim did not like being a slave.
    B. Huck wanted Jim to be his slave.
    C. Jim didn't trust Huck very much.
    D. Huck thought Jim needed new clothes.

_____ **3.** Which of these sentences is probably true?
    A. Shoes are a modern invention.
    B. Before Matzeliger's machine, shoes cost a lot.
    C. Everyone had to make their own shoes.
    D. People do not trust machines to do work.

_____ **4.** Which of these sentences is probably true?
    A. The American Red Cross started during the Civil War.
    B. Clara Barton spent her life helping people.
    C. Clara Barton never left the United States.
    D. Clara Barton never visited the United States.

_____ **5.** Which of these sentences is probably true?
    A. Rainbows are only seen in the west.
    B. Rainbows always appear during storms.
    C. Rainbows never appear when there are clouds.
    D. Rainbows rarely appear at night.

UNIT 3

1. A pet store owner in Maine noticed a strange thing. He found that he could tell when the country was having good times or bad. He looked at what kind of dogs people wanted to buy. People bought small dogs when they had enough money. People bought big dogs when they felt sad or needed protection.

2. Ichabod Crane listened politely as the old man spoke. His voice was full of fear. He told Crane about a ghost. It was called the Headless Horseman. The ghost scared people who entered a place called Sleepy Hollow after dark. Crane laughed to himself as he listened to the story. That night Crane took a short cut through Sleepy Hollow. Before he knew it, the ghost was chasing him.

3. The cowbird does not build a nest of its own. The mother cowbird lays her eggs in the nest of another bird. Then the cowbird leaves the eggs. She hopes the other bird will take care of her babies when they hatch.

4. The game was almost over. The Mudville team was losing, but Casey was the next batter. He was the best hitter on the team. The Mudville crowd roared as the pitcher threw one strike, then another. If Casey missed one more pitch, he would strike out. The pitcher threw again, and the Mudville crowd grew very quiet. Casey walked away from the plate.

5. Long ago, farmers watched animals to see when snow was coming. They thought snow would fall if a cat sneezed. Others felt that a dog with more fleas than usual was a sign of coming snow. Others watched for birds sitting high in the trees. That was a warning of snow, too.

_____ **1.** Which of these sentences is probably true?
- **A.** People bought big dogs during bad times.
- **B.** Pet store owners don't like dogs.
- **C.** People bought big dogs during good times.
- **D.** Dogs make better pets than cats do.

_____ **2.** Which of these sentences is probably true?
- **A.** The old man lived in Sleepy Hollow.
- **B.** Crane did not believe the man's story.
- **C.** Sleepy Hollow was far away.
- **D.** Crane liked to be chased.

_____ **3.** Which of these sentences is probably true?
- **A.** The cowbird is lazy.
- **B.** Nests are easy to build.
- **C.** The cowbird is very caring.
- **D.** Baby cowbirds eat much food.

_____ **4.** Which of these sentences is probably true?
- **A.** Casey hit the ball over the fence.
- **B.** The crowd forgot to cheer.
- **C.** Casey's team won the game.
- **D.** On the last pitch, Casey struck out.

_____ **5.** Which of these sentences is probably true?
- **A.** Farmers were happy when heavy snow fell.
- **B.** Most farmers enjoyed skiing and climbing mountains.
- **C.** Farmers thought birds could tell when snow was coming.
- **D.** Farmers did not have many dogs or cats.

1. Jim Smiley thought he was smarter than anyone else. Jim liked to be in contests, and he almost always won them. One day a new man arrived in town. This stranger offered to have a frog-jumping contest with Jim. Jim agreed and said he would find a good frog for the stranger. While Jim was gone, the stranger tied small weights to the legs of Jim's frog. Soon Jim returned with the stranger's frog.

2. The pyramids in Egypt were built more than 5,000 years ago. The pyramids are made of large blocks of stone. They are stacked on top of each other. The blocks are very heavy. People moved the blocks by placing logs under them. The logs acted like wheels to make the blocks easier to move. The stones were then pulled into place.

3. One day Ann heard her friend Tom talking. Tom was telling everybody how smart his dog was. Tom said his dog could do tricks and could even ride a bicycle. But Ann knew that Tom's dog was just like any other dog. So Ann just smiled as Tom went on talking.

4. Frogs and toads look very much alike. If you look closely, though, you will see many differences. Frogs have smooth and slimy skin. Toads have hard and rough skin. Frogs move by jumping. Toads walk or make short hops to move. Frogs live on land and in the water. Toads usually only live on land. By observing, it is easy to tell the difference between frogs and toads.

5. Fingernails grow faster on the right hand of people who are right-handed. The nails grow faster on the left hand of left-handed people. They grow faster in the day than at night. Ray has to trim the nails on his left hand more than the ones on his right hand.

_____ **1.** Which of these sentences is probably true?
  A. Jim's frog won the contest.
  B. The stranger's frog won the contest.
  C. Jim's frog jumped farther than it ever had.
  D. The frog tricked the stranger.

_____ **2.** Which of these sentences is probably true?
  A. The pyramids in Egypt are very old.
  B. The pyramids were built from large trees.
  C. Large rocks are easy to move.
  D. The pyramids were discovered recently.

_____ **3.** Which of these sentences is probably true?
  A. Ann didn't understand Tom's story.
  B. Tom wanted to make Ann mad at him.
  C. Ann didn't want to hurt Tom's feelings.
  D. Tom had two dogs and a cat.

_____ **4.** Which of these sentences is probably true?
  A. Toads are larger than frogs.
  B. Frogs do not jump.
  C. A toad has better hearing than a frog.
  D. A frog would live near a pond.

_____ **5.** Which of these sentences is probably true?
  A. Ray is a right-handed person.
  B. Painted nails grow very slowly.
  C. Ray is a left-handed person.
  D. At night Ray's nails grow quickly.

1. Shannon wanted to buy the doll she saw in the magazine. She begged her mother to give her the money. Shannon carefully wrote a letter to order the doll. Then she sent the letter in the mail. For weeks Shannon waited. Each day she hoped the doll would arrive. She knew the doll would be the best thing she had ever owned. At last the package arrived. But when Shannon opened the box, she found the doll broken into pieces.

2. The army ants of South America eat insects. These ants travel in groups. They sweep across the land in a dark bunch. People leave their homes for a while if they are in the ants' path.

3. Long ago in China, people had a strange idea about the world. They thought the world sat on the back of a giant frog. When the frog moved, the weather changed.

4. One day Sam found a library book under his bed. He realized he was late in taking it back. Sam decided to return the book the next day. But the next day, he could not find the book. Two days later Sam found the book again, so he hurried to the library. But when he arrived, there was a sign on the door. So he walked home again with the book in his hand.

5. King James had a plan. He wanted to make London the center of the silk business. He knew that silkworms made silk. People would pay lots of money for pretty silk clothes. The king planted a black mulberry tree at his palace. He told others in the land to plant the trees, too. He knew that silk worms ate many mulberry leaves. But there was one thing the king did not know. Silkworms would only eat the leaves of the white mulberry tree.

_____ **1.** Which of these sentences is probably true?
- **A.** Shannon cried when she opened the box.
- **B.** Getting the doll made Shannon happy.
- **C.** Shannon knew the doll would be broken.
- **D.** Shannon thought the broken doll was funny.

_____ **2.** Which of these sentences is probably true?
- **A.** People are really insects.
- **B.** The ants eat only plants.
- **C.** People return after the ants pass.
- **D.** The ants ride on trains.

_____ **3.** Which of these sentences is probably true?
- **A.** Long ago the world was smaller.
- **B.** The Chinese people had never seen frogs before.
- **C.** Long ago the weather was different.
- **D.** The Chinese people were trying to explain the weather.

_____ **4.** Which of these sentences is probably true?
- **A.** Sam didn't like the book very much.
- **B.** The book could move by itself.
- **C.** Sam did not know where the library was.
- **D.** When Sam went to the library, it was closed.

_____ **5.** Which of these sentences is probably true?
- **A.** Silkworms ate the black mulberry leaves.
- **B.** The king's plan didn't work out.
- **C.** London became the center of the silk business.
- **D.** The king moved to a new palace.

1. The day was sunny and hot. Ava stood happily at the side of the swimming pool. She thought about the clear, blue water. Then she jumped in. But as she began swimming, she started shaking, and her skin began to turn blue.

2. Laura Ingalls Wilder wrote about her life as a child. She lived with her Ma, Pa, and sister Mary. They lived in the Big Woods. The Big Woods went for miles and miles in all directions. Their log cabin was in a clearing in the trees. Laura had a garden behind the log cabin. She grew many different vegetables. Sometimes she found little tracks along the rows of vegetables. Deer had jumped the fence during the night. Her dog Jack chased the deer away.

3. Nick sat trembling behind the couch as a storm roared outside. Lightning flashed and thunder rumbled. Each time the thunder rolled, Nick screamed loudly. Nick's dad tried to get the boy to come out, but Nick would not move.

4. Six people in Maine came up with a plan. They wanted to help their high-school basketball team. They decided to bounce a basketball to the next town. Their team had its next game there. The December weather was cold and wet. But the six people did not let the bad weather stop them. They bounced the ball twenty miles to the next town. When they arrived they learned that the game would not be played. The weather was too bad.

5. After school on Thursday, Fred played video games. That night he watched TV and then read some magazines in his room. The next morning Fred walked slowly to his classroom. When the teacher passed out the test, the class began working. Fred stared at the questions. To him they seemed to be in a different language.

_____ **1.** Which of these sentences is probably true?
    A. The water was very hot.
    B. Ava forgot to wear her coat.
    C. The water was very cold.
    D. Ava didn't know how to swim.

_____ **2.** Which of these sentences is probably true?
    A. Laura's dog stayed inside at night.
    B. Deer like to eat vegetables.
    C. Laura's garden was far from the house.
    D. Laura's house had three bedrooms.

_____ **3.** Which of these sentences is probably true?
    A. Storms made Nick's dad afraid.
    B. Nick liked to play hide and seek.
    C. Nick's dad made him feel better.
    D. Nick was afraid of thunder and lightning.

_____ **4.** Which of these sentences is probably true?
    A. The six people were disappointed when
        they arrived.
    B. The basketball players didn't like the six people.
    C. Bouncing the ball in the cold was fun.
    D. The six people were glad no one showed up.

_____ **5.** Which of these sentences is probably true?
    A. The teacher passed out the wrong test.
    B. Fred did not do well on the test.
    C. The test was printed upside down.
    D. Fred did not need to study.

1. When his mother closed the door, Adam felt all alone. Adam was glad that the light by his bed was still on. Outside his window dark shadows danced in the night sky. He checked under his bed. Then he pulled the covers over his head. At last he was able to close his eyes and fall asleep.

2. Bill Stanton found a skunk in his garage. He asked the city of Chicago for help. He wanted to get rid of the skunk, but the city would not help him. So Bill bought a trap to catch the skunk himself. Then he learned he had broken the law several times. First he had brought a trap into the city. Then he had trapped an animal without the city's permission. The city laws stated that he could not keep the skunk in his garage. But they also said he could not kill the skunk or let it go free, either!

3. Tom Sawyer stared at the long, wooden fence. His aunt had ordered him to paint it. But just the thought of all that work made Tom tired. Then he had a wonderful idea. As he began to paint, he acted as if he was having lots of fun. Other boys began to watch. They wanted to have fun, too. Soon Tom had all the other boys doing his work for him.

4. During World War II, there wasn't enough rubber. So wooden tires for cars were tested. The wooden tires worked very well on smooth roads. But they cracked easily when they hit a hole.

5. The sport of softball began as indoor baseball. The first game of softball was played on a cold day in November 1887. It took place in a Chicago boat club. The men used an old boxing glove for a ball and a broomstick for a bat.

_____ **1.** Which of these sentences is probably true?
     A. Adam felt safe when his mom was in the room.
     B. Going to sleep was easy for Adam.
     C. The shadows outside did not scare Adam.
     D. Adam thought his mother was under the bed.

_____ **2.** Which of these sentences is probably true?
     A. The skunk became Bill's best friend.
     B. Bill didn't know what to do with the skunk.
     C. The skunk was moved to the city leaders' office.
     D. Bill was glad the skunk was in his garage.

_____ **3.** Which of these sentences is probably true?
     A. Working hard was fun for Tom.
     B. Tom didn't like fences.
     C. Tom's aunt painted the fence.
     D. Tom was a very tricky boy.

_____ **4.** Which of these sentences is probably true?
     A. Today wooden tires are still used.
     B. Making wooden tires was a good idea.
     C. Wooden tires did not replace rubber tires.
     D. The people who made wooden tires got rich.

_____ **5.** Which of these sentences is probably true?
     A. The men wanted to play baseball in the winter.
     B. Real baseballs cost a lot of money in 1887.
     C. The men didn't know how to play baseball.
     D. People first played softball outside.

1. Troy's dad had told him to come straight home after school. Troy was supposed to help his dad wash the car. But after school Troy talked to some friends for a while. On the way home, he stopped at the park to play basketball. When Troy finally got home, he saw that the car was already washed.

2. A town in California needed a footbridge. But the town leaders couldn't decide how to build it. They didn't know how much money to spend. One company said it would build the bridge for seven million dollars. The leaders talked about it for months. At last two boys decided to act. They built the bridge by themselves!

3. One day Kim went to the mall with her dad. First they visited a shoe store. Kim's dad just looked at the different shoes, but Kim bought two pairs. Then they decided to go to a toy store. There Kim bought a game and a soccer ball. Kim's dad soon got tired. He was ready to go home, but Kim wanted to look in several more stores.

4. When you think of dinosaurs, you likely think of large animals. Not all dinosaurs were large. The smallest dinosaurs were about the size of a chicken. They were fast runners. They probably ate insects, frogs, and lizards.

5. When Benjamin Franklin was a boy, he and his friends had an idea. They wanted to build a small dock to walk on. That way they could fish in the middle of the lake. They found a place to build it by the edge of the water. But they needed stones to build the dock. They found a pile of stones and started to work. Later the boys were surprised to learn that the stones had been gathered to build part of a new house.

_____ **1.** Which of these sentences is probably true?
    A. His dad didn't mind that Troy was late.
    B. Troy got in trouble for being late.
    C. His dad was glad that Troy had a good time.
    D. Troy had a special treat for supper.

_____ **2.** Which of these sentences is probably true?
    A. The boys liked to spend their own money.
    B. Building bridges was the boys' job.
    C. After one week the boys had finished the bridge.
    D. The boys got tired of waiting for the town's plan.

_____ **3.** Which of these sentences is probably true?
    A. Kim's family was very poor.
    B. Kim didn't like malls.
    C. Kim's dad was mean to her.
    D. Kim loved to go shopping.

_____ **4.** Which of these sentences is probably true?
    A. Dinosaurs were many different sizes.
    B. Dinosaurs ate only plants.
    C. Some dinosaurs looked like chickens.
    D. Dinosaurs were all about the same size.

_____ **5.** Which of these sentences is probably true?
    A. The workers helped the boys build the dock.
    B. Franklin lied about taking the stones.
    C. The workers were angry with the boys.
    D. The boys did not use the stones.

1. At last the time came for Amy to give her report. She had to stand in front of the whole class and tell them about spiders. As she stood up, she dropped her report. The pages scattered all across the floor. Amy could feel everyone staring at her as she picked up the mess. Finally she reached the front of the room. She looked out at the class. Amy could feel her face turning red. She tried to speak, but no words would come out of her mouth.

2. The speed limit on the road was 30 miles per hour. But drivers always went faster than that. The neighbors who lived on the road were angry about the speeders. So they talked to the city leaders. The leaders soon took action. They raised the speed limit to 35 miles per hour.

3. It was a cold day, and Ali stared at the white snow that covered the sidewalk. He knew he had a lot of shoveling to do. He was supposed to clean off the whole sidewalk. Out in the street, Ali's friends were pulling their sleds. Ali knew they were going to have fun sledding down the hill. They called for him to come, but Ali just waved. As they walked away, Ali slowly started to shovel.

4. If you are sick and you cough or sneeze on someone, that person could get sick, too. But it is not really a good idea to stop yourself from sneezing. If you do, you could pull a muscle in your face. You could also make your nose bleed.

5. Animals lose heat through their tails and ears. Animals that live in warm places have bigger ears and tails than those that live in cold places. A desert fox has long ears. But an arctic fox has short ears.

_____ **1.** Which of these sentences is probably true?
    A. Amy was in the wrong class.
    B. The class was afraid of Amy.
    C. Talking in front of people was hard for Amy.
    D. Amy knew nothing about spiders.

_____ **2.** Which of these sentences is probably true?
    A. The neighbors disliked the new speed limit.
    B. The neighbors were glad the leaders took action.
    C. After hearing the leaders' decision, the neighbors moved away.
    D. Drivers started going 30 miles per hour.

_____ **3.** Which of these sentences is probably true?
    A. Ali would rather work than play.
    B. The other children didn't like Ali.
    C. Ali loved to shovel snow.
    D. When Ali had a job to do, he did it.

_____ **4.** Which of these sentences is probably true?
    A. Sneezing makes your nose bleed.
    B. Stopping a sneeze could be harmful.
    C. You can get over a cold by not sneezing.
    D. Sneezing is good exercise for your face.

_____ **5.** Which of these sentences is probably true?
    A. Big ears help keep animals cool.
    B. Desert foxes have small tails.
    C. Animals with big ears eat healthier food.
    D. Arctic foxes need long ears.

1. Bob Hope was playing golf with a friend. His friend missed an easy shot. The angry friend threw his golf club into the tall grass. Bob secretly got the golf club back and started using it himself. Bob hit the ball a long way with his friend's club. The friend thought Bob's golf club was very good. He offered to buy it for fifty dollars. Bob sold the man the club he had just thrown away. Later Bob told his friend what had happened.

2. Jo's mom was in the hospital. She had just had a new baby. Jo had seen the little baby boy with his wrinkled skin and his funny face. Jo was excited to have a new brother. But she was worried that her parents might not love her anymore.

3. The President was coming to visit the small town. Everyone was very excited. All the people worked hard to clean up their town. They mowed the grass and swept the sidewalks. They fixed up the old houses. They even painted the water tower.

4. Morgan's dad had gone to have the car fixed. Morgan couldn't believe how much old stuff was piled up in the garage. Morgan stared at it for a while, and then he knew what he had to do. The garage was filled with noise and dust that afternoon. But when Morgan's dad arrived home with the car, the garage was as clean as could be.

5. Samuel Clemens grew up near the Mississippi River. As a boy he played by the river for hours. He watched the water change colors as the sun moved through the sky. When he got older, Clemens got a job as a riverboat pilot. He later changed his name to Mark Twain. His new name came from a saying that riverboat pilots used. The saying told how deep the water was.

_____ **1.** Which of these sentences is probably true?
    A. Bob decided to keep his friend's golf club.
    B. Bob's friend felt silly for buying back his own club.
    C. Bob used the money to open a golf shop.
    D. Bob's friend never played golf again.

_____ **2.** Which of these sentences is probably true?
    A. Jo's parents needed to tell her they could love two children.
    B. Jo did not like wrinkles or funny faces.
    C. Jo's mother was at home.
    D. Jo wanted a dog instead of a new baby brother.

_____ **3.** Which of these sentences is probably true?
    A. The President was moving to the town.
    B. The people were trying to fool the President.
    C. The President only liked big towns.
    D. The people wanted their town to look nice.

_____ **4.** Which of these sentences is probably true?
    A. Morgan liked fixing cars.
    B. Morgan's father had been sick.
    C. Morgan was a hard worker.
    D. Morgan's father liked dirty garages.

_____ **5.** Which of these sentences is probably true?
    A. Clemens loved the river.
    B. The other pilots didn't like Clemens.
    C. Clemens could not swim.
    D. The river always looked the same.

1. Jim carefully lifted the eggs from their box. He handed two eggs to his mother. Then Jim measured a cup of milk, being careful not to spill any. He rubbed the pan with butter and watched as his mother poured in the batter. Then Jim and his mother cleaned up.

2. Marion Morrison was born in 1907. He grew up in a small town in Iowa. When he got older, he moved to California. There he began to make movies. He often played the part of a tough cowboy. He decided to change his name. His new name was John Wayne. He soon became a famous star.

3. Jan was always playing basketball. In fact, she almost never left the basketball court. Jan started practicing early every morning. As the sun went down, Jan was still bouncing the basketball.

4. Nan was helping her uncle on the farm. He was loading the truck with hay for the cows. Nan's uncle threw a rope over the bales of hay. He told Nan to tie the rope carefully. But Nan only tied a loose knot. Then she hurried off to get a cool drink.

5. When Babe Ruth was a boy, he was very poor. He had many problems. He got in fights with other boys, and often he lost. At last he was sent to St. Mary's School. There he met Brother Gilbert. Brother Gilbert discovered the one thing that would keep Babe out of trouble. He introduced Babe to baseball.

_____ **1.** Which of these sentences is probably true?
      A. Jim was a good helper.
      B. Jim's mother was a bad cook.
      C. Jim was hungry.
      D. Jim's mother was lazy.

_____ **2.** Which of these sentences is probably true?
      A. Marion's mother was named Mrs. Wayne.
      B. Marion changed his name to Sam.
      C. Marion's father was a tough cowboy.
      D. Marion thought John Wayne was a better name for a cowboy.

_____ **3.** Which of these sentences is probably true?
      A. Jan slept at the basketball court.
      B. Tennis was very important to Jan.
      C. Jan wanted to be a great basketball player.
      D. The basketball was too big to bounce inside.

_____ **4.** Which of these sentences is probably true?
      A. All the cool drinks were already gone.
      B. The rope tightened itself.
      C. The knot came untied.
      D. The cool drink made Nan sick.

_____ **5.** Which of these sentences is probably true?
      A. Baseball got Babe Ruth in trouble.
      B. Babe Ruth loved playing baseball.
      C. Baseball made Babe Ruth poor.
      D. Babe Ruth liked fighting more than playing baseball.

1. During World War II, young Anne Frank had a hard life. Her family had to hide from the German soldiers. They stayed in one small room. Anne was afraid day after day. To make herself feel better, she wrote about her feelings. One day she wrote, "In spite of everything, I still believe that people are really good at heart."

2. Jack walked slowly toward town, pulling his cow behind him. Jack and his mother were very poor. He was supposed to sell the cow for money to buy food. Along the way Jack met a funny little man. The man offered to trade some magic beans for Jack's cow. The man said the beans could make Jack happy. So Jack traded the cow for the beans.

3. When he was a boy, George Washington Carver had a garden. He loved to study the plants and flowers growing there. He knew how to make the flowers bloom. George could also cure sick plants. People began to call him the "plant doctor."

4. Greyfriars Bobby was a dog. He belonged to a policeman named Jock Gray. Bobby and Jock were great friends. When Jock died, Bobby watched over the ground where Jock was buried. Bobby stayed close to the grave until he died.

5. Orville and Wilbur Wright loved to build things. When they were small, the brothers made paper toys that would fly. When they got older, they opened a bicycle shop. One day they thought about the flying toys they had made. They started trying to build a flying machine. They studied birds flying and made many models. At last their machine was complete. In 1903 Orville climbed into the machine and took off. Wilbur smiled with pride.

_____ **1.** Which of these sentences is probably true?
  A. Hiding in the little room was fun for Anne.
  B. Anne tried to think about the good things in life.
  C. Writing in the notebook was scary for Anne.
  D. Anne didn't think she had any problems.

_____ **2.** Which of these sentences is probably true?
  A. Jack did not like the cow.
  B. The cow wanted to go with the man.
  C. Jack believed in magic.
  D. The man was Jack's friend.

_____ **3.** Which of these sentences is probably true?
  A. George became a plant scientist later in life.
  B. The neighbors didn't like George's garden.
  C. George chopped down all the plants.
  D. His mother called George the "animal doctor."

_____ **4.** Which of these sentences is probably true?
  A. Bobby couldn't find his way home.
  B. Jock had been good to Bobby.
  C. Bobby never got hungry.
  D. Jock didn't have many friends.

_____ **5.** Which of these sentences is probably true?
  A. Their flying machine was made of feathers.
  B. The Wright brothers fought a lot.
  C. Birds scared the Wright brothers.
  D. The Wright brothers loved flying.

Writing

Read each story. Then read the question that follows it. Write your answers on the lines below each question.

1. Karen watered the rose plant. It was in a pot. Then she spotted water leaking under the pot. She did not want water stains on the shelf. So she put some old newspapers under the pot. As she did this, the sun hit her and the rose. Tomorrow the rose would be in a new pot.

Where did Karen keep the flowerpot?

_____

_____

2. Leon pulled his pencil out of the sharpener. Then he shook the shavings off the pencil. It looked fine. He was ready to start writing again.

Why did Leon stop writing?

_____

_____

3. The dog looked up and down the street. The man waited until the dog stepped off the curb. Then the man followed the dog. They crossed the street.

Why did the man wait for the dog?

_____

_____

To check your answers, turn to page 60.

Read the paragraph below. Then answer the questions.

Mary grew six inches in her first year in high school. Now she wants to join the basketball team. Mary knows she must build her skills over the summer. So every day she practices her shooting and dribbling. Some days she gets her little brother to help. She practices passing the ball to him. Soon Mary plans to visit the playground. There she can practice with players who are on the team. She can learn how she is doing. She can also find out what else she needs to learn.

1. Why didn't Mary join the team in her first year?

_____

_____

2. What skill does Mary's little brother need to help Mary?

_____

_____

3. What kind of person is Mary?

_____

_____

4. How does Mary feel about her skills?

_____

_____

To check your answers, turn to page 60.

Inference • Level C

1. Shoes were not always made differently for right and left feet. For hundreds of years, shoemakers made shoes to fit either foot. After shoes were worn for a while, the leather would stretch to fit the right or left foot. Around 1850 special sewing machines made it easier to produce shoes. Several years after that, shoes were made for each foot.

2. Betty Graham was a secretary. She typed many pages. When she made a mistake, she had to start over. She found that white paint would cover up mistakes. Then she could just type over the mistake. This saved her much time. She made a special paint that worked better. She made a lot of money from her invention.

3. Jenna sat alone at the lunch table. It was her first day at the new school. Katie, a girl in Jenna's class, was sitting at another table with her friends. She noticed Jenna eating lunch by herself. Katie walked over to the table where Jenna was sitting.

4. People have been eating cheese for over 4,000 years. Cheese is made from milk. As milk turns to cheese, solid clumps form. When the liquid is taken out, the cheese becomes even harder. The cheese is then allowed to *age*. This means it has to sit for a while before it's ready. Sometimes the cheese is ready to be eaten in two weeks. For other types of cheese, aging takes up to two years.

5. For hundreds of years corks have been used to seal bottles. Corks are really the bark of a tree. They are not from just any tree. They are from a type of oak tree. The cork oak grows in Spain. The thick bark of the tree is peeled off in large sheets. The corks are cut from the sheets. The bark of each tree can be cut off every eight years.

Fact	Inference	
○	○	**1.** **A.** Shoes stretched to fit each foot.
○	○	**B.** Shoes were made of stretchy material.
○	○	**C.** Leather can stretch.
○	○	**D.** Shoes were made to fit either foot.

Fact	Inference	
○	○	**2.** **A.** White paint can cover up mistakes.
○	○	**B.** Painting over mistakes saves time.
○	○	**C.** Betty Graham sold her special paint.
○	○	**D.** Betty Graham made a special paint to hide mistakes.

Fact	Inference	
○	○	**3.** **A.** Katie cared how Jenna felt.
○	○	**B.** It was Jenna's first day at school.
○	○	**C.** Katie walked to Jenna's table.
○	○	**D.** Jenna was lonely.

Fact	Inference	
○	○	**4.** **A.** Cheese is made from milk.
○	○	**B.** There are different kinds of cheeses.
○	○	**C.** Aging cheese can take two years.
○	○	**D.** Cheese hardens when liquid is removed.

Fact	Inference	
○	○	**5.** **A.** Corks are made from the bark of an oak tree.
○	○	**B.** The bark of a cork oak grows slowly.
○	○	**C.** The bark is peeled off the tree.
○	○	**D.** Many corks can be made from the bark of each tree.

1. Have you ever caught fireflies on a warm summer night? Fireflies are interesting little insects. They make light with their bodies. But the light is not hot. Fireflies use their lights to send signals to other fireflies.

2. A long time ago, no one knew that dinosaurs had ever lived. But in 1822 an English woman found a large tooth. In a few years, other parts of these large reptiles known as dinosaurs were found.

3. William loved to go fishing. His grandfather had promised to take him on Saturday. That morning William packed a lunch and got his fishing pole ready. But about an hour before it was time to go, the phone rang. His grandfather said he was not feeling well and couldn't take William fishing. William was disappointed, but decided to make his grandfather a get-well card.

4. Long ago, people gathered wild plants and hunted wild animals for food. At first people hunted only small animals. Later, they learned ways of catching larger animals. Half a million years ago, people learned to make fire. Before that they had to take burning wood from fires that had started naturally. When people learned to make their own fires, they began to cook some of their food.

5. It had been raining all day. Maria splashed through a puddle on her way home from school. As she came to her house, her dad opened the door. Maria quickly took off her raincoat. "Look, Maria," he said. "There's a surprise for you." A fuzzy kitten looked up at her from the rug.

Fact	Inference	
○	○	**1.** **A.** Fireflies come out in summer.
○	○	**B.** The light of fireflies is not hot.
○	○	**C.** Fireflies send signals with their lights.
○	○	**D.** Fireflies can only send signals at night.

Fact	Inference	
○	○	**2.** **A.** Dinosaurs lived before 1822.
○	○	**B.** Dinosaur bones were first found in England.
○	○	**C.** A tooth was the first dinosaur bone found.
○	○	**D.** Dinosaurs were reptiles.

Fact	Inference	
○	○	**3.** **A.** William was a caring person.
○	○	**B.** William loved to go fishing.
○	○	**C.** William loved his grandfather.
○	○	**D.** William's grandfather was sick.

Fact	Inference	
○	○	**4.** **A.** People hunted wild animals.
○	○	**B.** Large animals were hard to catch.
○	○	**C.** Fire was important to early people.
○	○	**D.** Some food was cooked over a fire.

Fact	Inference	
○	○	**5.** **A.** Maria took off her raincoat.
○	○	**B.** It was a rainy day.
○	○	**C.** Maria walked through a puddle.
○	○	**D.** Maria's dad got a kitten for her.

1. George Bidder was different from most boys his age. He was a whiz at math. When he was asked to work a math problem, he could do it in his head. Once he was told a 43-digit number backward. Right away he was able to switch it around in his head and say it forward in its correct order. He could even remember the number an hour later!

2. The city was full of people on their way home. Buses, trucks, cars, and taxis crowded the streets. Mark was in a hurry to catch the bus. As he ran up to the bus stop, the bus roared away. Mark sat down on a nearby bench and frowned.

3. If you watch the sky at night, you may see a shooting star. Shooting stars are actually meteors. Meteors are small bits of rock that enter the atmosphere. When this happens, they burn up. They look like streaks of light. Sometimes the Earth passes through a place with many small rocks. When this happens, the sky is filled with meteors. Because there are so many, these are called meteor showers.

4. Robert Fulton built the first steamboat. His first try did not go very well. The boat sank to the bottom of the river. It was very heavy. A few years later, in 1807, he tried again. This time his boat, the *Clermont*, made a successful trip down the Hudson River in New York.

5. Drew's team was tied with the other soccer team. The game was almost over. Drew had scored all his team's goals in the game so far. His friend Brian had never scored a goal. As Drew ran up the field, he saw that Brian was in a great position to kick the ball into the goal. Drew quickly kicked the ball to Brian.

Fact	Inference	
○	○	**1. A.** George worked math problems in his head.
○	○	**B.** Math was George's favorite subject.
○	○	**C.** George was a math whiz.
○	○	**D.** People thought George was very smart.

Fact	Inference	
○	○	**2. A.** Mark ran to catch the bus.
○	○	**B.** Mark was angry he missed the bus.
○	○	**C.** The city streets were crowded.
○	○	**D.** Mark was on his way home.

Fact	Inference	
○	○	**3. A.** Meteors are small bits of rock.
○	○	**B.** Meteors are not really stars.
○	○	**C.** Most meteors never reach the ground.
○	○	**D.** Meteor showers are made up of many meteors.

Fact	Inference	
○	○	**4. A.** Robert Fulton did not give up easily.
○	○	**B.** Fulton's boat was called the *Clermont*.
○	○	**C.** The *Clermont* did not sink.
○	○	**D.** The first boat was very heavy.

Fact	Inference	
○	○	**5. A.** Drew wanted Brian to make a goal.
○	○	**B.** Drew was a thoughtful person.
○	○	**C.** Drew was a good soccer player.
○	○	**D.** Brian had never scored a goal.

1. It gets much hotter and much colder on the moon than here on Earth. At noon the temperature is four times higher on the moon than on Earth. For two weeks the moon stays dark all day long. This is called lunar night. At that time it is four times colder than on Earth.

2. Miguel kicked the rocks in front of his feet. He had been excited about going to the rodeo. He wanted to see the cowboys do tricks. But now his mother wanted him to finish his farm work first. He slowly walked to the barn to water the horses. Then his brother's friend Ravon drove up in a truck. "How would you like a ride to the rodeo?" he asked.

3. Mount St. Helens is a volcano in Washington. In 1980 it erupted for the first time in more than one hundred years. Fire and melting rock poured out of the volcano. This caused rivers to flood. Four states were covered with ash. More than sixty people were killed.

4. Ching and her mother were shopping for groceries. While they were waiting at the checkout line, her mother realized she had forgotten something. She turned to Ching and asked, "Could you go get me some eggs, please?" Ching ran to get the eggs. As she was coming back, she did not notice the wet floor.

5. Marta and her cousin Pilar set up a lawn-mowing service. They had made quite a bit of money over the summer. Mr. Lee was their neighbor. He had been sick lately, and his lawn had not been mowed. Marta and Pilar decided to mow the lawn for him. When Mr. Lee offered to pay them, they wouldn't take his money.

Fact	Inference	
○	○	**1. A.** The moon is coldest during lunar night.
○	○	**B.** Lunar night lasts two weeks.
○	○	**C.** The moon is hotter and colder than Earth.
○	○	**D.** It is hottest on the moon at noon.

Fact	Inference	
○	○	**2. A.** The horses were thirsty.
○	○	**B.** Miguel was excited about going to the rodeo.
○	○	**C.** Ravon drove up in a truck.
○	○	**D.** Miguel did not finish his work.

Fact	Inference	
○	○	**3. A.** Mount St. Helens erupted in 1980.
○	○	**B.** The volcano did not erupt often.
○	○	**C.** People lived near Mount St. Helens.
○	○	**D.** Mount St. Helens is in Washington.

Fact	Inference	
○	○	**4. A.** Ching fell down on the floor.
○	○	**B.** Someone had spilled water on the floor.
○	○	**C.** Ching's mother asked her to get eggs.
○	○	**D.** Ching was helpful.

Fact	Inference	
○	○	**5. A.** Marta and Pilar wanted to help Mr. Lee.
○	○	**B.** Mr. Lee had been sick lately.
○	○	**C.** Marta and Pilar were hard workers.
○	○	**D.** Mr. Lee offered to pay the girls.

1. The moon was full. The sea air smelled fresh and clean. Sue and her mom decided to take a walk. Sue pushed her mom's wheelchair along the sidewalk. They could see the ocean in the distance. They stopped often to look up at the stars. The last few days of getting ready for their vacation had been very busy. Now it was time to have fun.

2. Popcorn is one of the oldest kinds of corn. It was first grown by people in North and South America. Today most popcorn is grown in Nebraska and Indiana.

3. Dana loved computers. Once or twice a week, she went to the computer store near her house. The owner was glad to let Dana use the computers, but he told her not to bring drinks inside. One day Dana carried a can of apple juice into the store.

4. Mammoths lived thousands of years ago. They looked a little like elephants. They had trunks and long teeth called tusks. Some had hair all over their bodies. They were called woolly mammoths. The bones of mammoths have been found in Siberia. The last mammoths died about ten thousand years ago.

5. Sean and Matt were friends. They had been practicing for the school play. They both wanted to play the part of Robin Hood. When Mrs. Gray called the list of actors, Sean found out that Matt would get to play Robin Hood. Sean didn't play with Matt after school that day. He stayed alone in his room.

Fact	Inference	
○	○	**1.** **A.** Sue and her mom were on vacation.
○	○	**B.** It was night.
○	○	**C.** Sue and her mom liked being together.
○	○	**D.** The stars were bright.

Fact	Inference	
○	○	**2.** **A.** Popcorn is grown in Indiana.
○	○	**B.** People in South America grew popcorn.
○	○	**C.** Popcorn doesn't grow well everywhere.
○	○	**D.** People still eat popcorn.

Fact	Inference	
○	○	**3.** **A.** Dana spilled the apple juice.
○	○	**B.** The owner was angry with Dana.
○	○	**C.** Dana liked apple juice.
○	○	**D.** The store was near Dana's house.

Fact	Inference	
○	○	**4.** **A.** Woolly mammoths had hair on their bodies.
○	○	**B.** Mammoths had trunks and tusks.
○	○	**C.** Woolly mammoths died long ago.
○	○	**D.** Mammoths lived in Siberia.

Fact	Inference	
○	○	**5.** **A.** Sean wanted to play Robin Hood.
○	○	**B.** Matt was a better actor than Sean.
○	○	**C.** Sean was sad he didn't get the part.
○	○	**D.** Matt got the part of Robin Hood.

1. Andy watched his mother take his training wheels off. He was excited to try out his bike. But without the training wheels, he kept falling off. Then his older brother Jeff came outside. Jeff had an idea. He ran beside Andy as Andy pedaled the bike. Andy rode faster and faster. Soon Jeff couldn't keep up. Andy was riding the bike by himself!

2. Mushrooms grow under piles of fallen leaves or on dead logs. People eat mushrooms in spaghetti or on pizza, but not all mushrooms are good to eat. Some mushrooms have poison in them. The poisonous ones are called toadstools.

3. Juan likes to help his grandmother make tamales. Tamales are ground corn dough with a spicy filling. Making them takes a long time. First, his grandmother makes the dough and the filling. Then, she places the dough and filling on a corn shuck. Juan's job is to wrap the tamales. He rolls them up. Then they are cooked. The tamales are unwrapped just before eating.

4. Dimes are sometimes called silver coins. This is because of their color. Before 1964, dimes contained silver. Silver did not cost much. Then it became valuable. Soon, the silver was worth more than ten cents. So dimes were made with a cheaper metal. Today, dimes are still the same color. They just don't have any silver.

5. Oseola McCarty worked hard. She washed and ironed clothes. She never went to college. For 75 years she saved her money. In 1995 she gave $150,000 to a college. The money was to help poor African American students. Her money helped them pay for school. She wanted to help others. She has given many students a chance. She hoped that college could change their lives.

Fact	Inference	
◯	◯	**1.** **A.** Andy fell off his bike.
◯	◯	**B.** Jeff wanted to help Andy.
◯	◯	**C.** Andy's mother took off his training wheels.
◯	◯	**D.** Jeff was Andy's older brother.

Fact	Inference	
◯	◯	**2.** **A.** Some mushrooms are poisonous.
◯	◯	**B.** People eat mushrooms on pizza.
◯	◯	**C.** Mushrooms grow on dead logs.
◯	◯	**D.** People should not eat toadstools.

Fact	Inference	
◯	◯	**3.** **A.** Tamales must be unwrapped before eating.
◯	◯	**B.** Juan's family enjoys tamales.
◯	◯	**C.** Tamales are wrapped in corn shucks.
◯	◯	**D.** Tamales have spicy filling.

Fact	Inference	
◯	◯	**4.** **A.** Silver is a valuable metal.
◯	◯	**B.** Dimes used to be made of silver.
◯	◯	**C.** Dimes are not made of valuable metal today.
◯	◯	**D.** Today's dimes only look like silver.

Fact	Inference	
◯	◯	**5.** **A.** McCarty gave most of her money to a college.
◯	◯	**B.** McCarty wanted others to go to college.
◯	◯	**C.** McCarty washed and ironed clothes.
◯	◯	**D.** Giving money to the college made McCarty happy.

1. José had been sick for a week. He had chicken pox. His teacher asked if anyone in the class could take José's homework to him. Dave had already had chicken pox, so he raised his hand. On his way to José's house, he bought some baseball cards for José.

2. People have used wheels for over five thousand years. They were probably first used in Middle Eastern countries. Chinese people learned to use the wheel about two thousand years later. Native Americans did not use wheels for work at that time. But they did put wheels on their toys.

3. Carlos Finlay was a Cuban doctor. He saw many cases of yellow fever. No one knew what caused yellow fever. No one knew how to cure it. Finlay wanted to find the cause and a cure. He found that whatever caused it was carried by mosquitoes. He did not find a cure for yellow fever. But his work did show that by stopping mosquito bites, people could stop the illness.

4. Gold was found in Georgia many years ago. At that time mostly Cherokee people lived there. White settlers wanted the gold and the land. With the help of the United States government, they forced the Cherokees to move west. Thousands of Cherokees died on the march to Oklahoma. It was called the Trail of Tears.

5. Benito Juárez is a hero in Mexico. He was born in a poor Indian village. He worked hard. He went to college and studied law. He wanted to make Mexico a free country. He worked in the government to free Mexico. His country won its freedom from France. In 1861 he became the first Indian president of Mexico. Juárez showed that he was a great leader.

Fact	Inference	
○	○	**1.** **A.** Dave and José were friends.
○	○	**B.** José had chicken pox.
○	○	**C.** Dave raised his hand.
○	○	**D.** José liked baseball cards.

Fact	Inference	
○	○	**2.** **A.** Some Native American toys had wheels.
○	○	**B.** People in China used wheels to do work.
○	○	**C.** China is not in the Middle East.
○	○	**D.** Wheels have been used for a long time.

Fact	Inference	
○	○	**3.** **A.** Yellow fever is carried by mosquitoes.
○	○	**B.** Mosquitoes carry the illness from person to person.
○	○	**C.** Dr. Finlay found how to stop yellow fever.
○	○	**D.** Yellow fever makes people sick.

Fact	Inference	
○	○	**4.** **A.** Gold was found in Georgia.
○	○	**B.** The settlers wanted the land.
○	○	**C.** The march to Oklahoma was long.
○	○	**D.** The Cherokees were forced to move west.

Fact	Inference	
○	○	**5.** **A.** Benito Juárez worked hard to become president.
○	○	**B.** Benito Juárez gave people hope.
○	○	**C.** Benito Juárez was an Indian.
○	○	**D.** Benito Juárez became president of Mexico.

1. One man made a pizza so big it could feed thirty thousand people. The pizza was over one hundred feet across. It was cut into over ninety thousand slices! The man's name was Mr. Avato. He set a world record.

2. "Don't you ever come here again!" Rosa shouted to her best friend Gail. "Don't you worry. I won't!" Gail shouted back. Gail slammed the front door shut as she left. After a few minutes, Rosa was sorry for what she had said. She ran out the front door and headed toward Gail's house. Gail was running down the sidewalk to Rosa's house.

3. Have you ever wondered what it would be like to live in another country? Each year thousands of American students do just that. They live in another country for a few months. Some even stay for a year. They live with a host family in the new country. The host family members try to make the student a part of their family life. The students go to school, make friends, visit new places, and eat new foods. Sometimes they even learn to speak another language.

4. Rob heard a rooster crow. He opened his eyes and felt the sun shining through the window. It was his first day on his cousin's farm. He jumped out of bed and began putting on his jeans. When his aunt called him to breakfast, he ran downstairs eagerly.

5. Think about this the next time you brush your teeth. Before people had toothbrushes, they used twigs. They would smash the end to make it like a brush. About 600 years ago, the toothbrush was invented in China. It was made from hog hair. Hog hairs are very stiff and are called bristles. The bristles were attached to a wooden stick. Today, toothbrushes are not made with hog hairs. They have nylon bristles.

Fact	Inference	
○	○	**1. A.** The pizza was over 100 feet across.
○	○	**B.** The pizza set a world record.
○	○	**C.** Mr. Avato likes pizza.
○	○	**D.** There were over ninety thousand pieces.

Fact	Inference	
○	○	**2. A.** Rosa and Gail were best friends.
○	○	**B.** Gail was coming to say she was sorry.
○	○	**C.** Rosa shouted at Gail.
○	○	**D.** Gail slammed the front door.

Fact	Inference	
○	○	**3. A.** Most host families speak English.
○	○	**B.** Some students learn a new language.
○	○	**C.** Host families like Americans.
○	○	**D.** The students visit new places.

Fact	Inference	
○	○	**4. A.** Rob liked farm life.
○	○	**B.** The sun was shining.
○	○	**C.** Rob was hungry.
○	○	**D.** A rooster crowed.

Fact	Inference	
○	○	**5. A.** Toothbrushes have changed over time.
○	○	**B.** People first used twigs to clean their teeth.
○	○	**C.** Modern toothbrushes have nylon bristles.
○	○	**D.** The first toothbrushes used wooden sticks and hog hair.

UNIT 21

1. Emma heard someone crying for help. She ran down toward the lake. A boy was splashing around wildly. In a flash Emma ran to get the rope that hung on a tree nearby. She threw it once, but the boy missed it. She walked a little way into the cold water and tried again. This time she could feel the boy pull on the other end.

2. No one really knows what happened to the first English settlers in the New World. Their leader, John White, left them to go to England for supplies. When he returned over a year later, the settlers were gone. Some people think they were killed. Others think they may have gone to live with a friendly Native American tribe. We will probably never solve the mystery of the "Lost Colony."

3. It was a warm, windy day. Tina and Luis went to fly their kite. "Find a good spot this time," their mother said. "Remember what happened when you flew your kite over by the woods." But the open field was very far away, and Tina and Luis were in a hurry. They walked toward the woods.

4. The Eagles were tied with the Wildcats. There were only three seconds left in the game. The Eagles' best player had the ball. He bounced it once before he jumped up to make the shot. Everyone was quiet as they watched the ball fly toward the basket. Then the Eagle fans jumped up and yelled, "All right!"

5. Sally Ride was the first American woman to travel in space. In 1983 she made a flight that lasted six days. The flight was made on the space shuttle *Challenger*. The next year she made another flight. She studied Earth's weather.

Fact	Inference	
◯	◯	**1.** **A.** Emma saved the boy.
◯	◯	**B.** The boy was drowning in the lake.
◯	◯	**C.** Emma knew where a rope was.
◯	◯	**D.** Emma heard someone crying for help.

Fact	Inference	
◯	◯	**2.** **A.** The settlers needed supplies.
◯	◯	**B.** John White was the leader of the group.
◯	◯	**C.** Some people think the settlers were killed.
◯	◯	**D.** No one really knows what happened.

Fact	Inference	
◯	◯	**3.** **A.** Tina and Luis went to fly a kite.
◯	◯	**B.** Windy days are good for flying kites.
◯	◯	**C.** Tina and Luis were in a hurry.
◯	◯	**D.** Last time their kite got stuck in a tree.

Fact	Inference	
◯	◯	**4.** **A.** The Eagles were a basketball team.
◯	◯	**B.** The score was tied.
◯	◯	**C.** The Eagles won the game.
◯	◯	**D.** There were three seconds left in the game.

Fact	Inference	
◯	◯	**5.** **A.** Sally Ride traveled in space.
◯	◯	**B.** The *Challenger* was a space shuttle.
◯	◯	**C.** Sally Ride was interested in science.
◯	◯	**D.** Sally Ride studied the weather.

1. The Vikings were probably the first Europeans to find North America. Ruins of Viking houses have been found in Newfoundland. Their houses were built around A.D. 1000. English fishers probably didn't reach that area until 1481. Columbus thought he was the first one to find the New World in 1492.

2. You may have seen ants carry big things. Ants can lift 50 times their body weight. This means that ants are very strong. Bees are even stronger. Bees can lift 300 times their body weight. To be as strong as a bee, a person would have to lift 15 tons! Are you as strong as a bee?

3. Sitting Bull was born in South Dakota. He became a Sioux chief. It was a very hard time for his people. White settlers were moving onto Sioux land. In 1868 the United States asked the Sioux and Cheyenne chiefs to sign a peace treaty. Many chiefs signed the treaty and lived on the reservation. But Sitting Bull did not. He wanted to live the old way.

4. When we think of windmills, we often think of Holland. The people there used windmills to take water off their land. That way they had more land for farming. Now windmills are used to make electricity.

5. A compass is used as a guide. The needle of a compass always points north. The needle is really just a small magnet. The needle is balanced so that it turns freely. When the compass is turned, the needle continues to point north. The compass was invented in China about 2,000 years ago. It was used to guide ships on long trips.

Fact	Inference	
○	○	**1. A.** Vikings built houses about A.D. 1000.
○	○	**B.** Newfoundland is in North America.
○	○	**C.** Columbus didn't reach the New World first.
○	○	**D.** Columbus didn't know about the Vikings.

Fact	Inference	
○	○	**2. A.** Bees are stronger than humans.
○	○	**B.** A person cannot lift 15 tons.
○	○	**C.** Bees are stronger than ants.
○	○	**D.** Ants can lift 50 times their body weight.

Fact	Inference	
○	○	**3. A.** Sitting Bull was a Sioux chief.
○	○	**B.** Sitting Bull did not like the white settlers.
○	○	**C.** Sitting Bull did not sign the treaty.
○	○	**D.** Sitting Bull did not want to change.

Fact	Inference	
○	○	**4. A.** There is not enough farmland in Holland.
○	○	**B.** Farmland must be fairly dry.
○	○	**C.** Holland has many windmills.
○	○	**D.** Now windmills make electricity.

Fact	Inference	
○	○	**5. A.** If a compass is turned, the needle still points one direction.
○	○	**B.** A compass could help a ship when it is cloudy.
○	○	**C.** A compass always points north.
○	○	**D.** Ship captains found the compass helpful.

1. The English Channel flows between France and England. At least 228 people have swum the 21-mile crossing. Some crossings may have been in secret. Police think a French soldier crossed the channel in 1815. He escaped from a prison in Dover, England.

2. Pam was in the hospital. Her class wanted to show Pam that they missed her. "I have an idea," Emily said. "Let's make a big banner for Pam." The class spent the morning making the banner. It said, "The kids at Brook School care about you!" They asked other students in the school to sign it, too.

3. Did you ever hear of the Underground Railroad? It wasn't a real railroad. But it did carry slaves to their freedom. It was run by people like Harriet Tubman. She had once been a slave, too. Slaves who were running away were told about safe places to stay. Harriet Tubman helped over three hundred slaves escape to freedom.

4. Alex's dad had lost his job. His family did not have much money. One afternoon Alex and his dad were walking near their home. Alex ran ahead to see a squirrel. Then suddenly he saw something under a leaf. He pulled it out and saw that it was a twenty-dollar bill. Alex thought of all the things he would like to buy. But he turned around. "Come here, Dad," he said.

5. Henry Ford was one of America's first carmakers. He found ways to make cars cost less. Many people couldn't buy other cars, which cost more. But most Americans had enough money to buy Ford's Model T. The Ford Motor Company sold 15 million Model T's in less than 20 years.

Fact	Inference	
◯	◯	**1.** **A.** A soldier escaped from prison.
◯	◯	**B.** The channel is filled with water.
◯	◯	**C.** The prison was near the channel.
◯	◯	**D.** The channel is 21 miles wide.

Fact	Inference	
◯	◯	**2.** **A.** Pam needed to be cheered up.
◯	◯	**B.** The students made a banner.
◯	◯	**C.** Emily took the banner to Pam.
◯	◯	**D.** The students signed the banner.

Fact	Inference	
◯	◯	**3.** **A.** Slaves were told about safe places to stay.
◯	◯	**B.** Harriet Tubman was once a slave.
◯	◯	**C.** People didn't like being slaves.
◯	◯	**D.** Harriet Tubman cared about slaves.

Fact	Inference	
◯	◯	**4.** **A.** Alex gave his dad the money.
◯	◯	**B.** The money was under a leaf.
◯	◯	**C.** Alex wanted to help his father.
◯	◯	**D.** Alex's dad had lost his job.

Fact	Inference	
◯	◯	**5.** **A.** Other cars cost more than the Model T.
◯	◯	**B.** Henry Ford was a smart businessperson.
◯	◯	**C.** Fifteen million Model T's were sold.
◯	◯	**D.** Americans liked Model T's.

1. The Venus's-flytrap is a strange plant. An insect that flies near it doesn't have much of a chance. When an insect touches the leaves in the center of the plant, the leaves snap shut. The insect gets trapped inside. It takes a few days for the Venus's-flytrap to finish eating the insect.

2. Ben and his dad were out running. Suddenly there was a loud crack of thunder. Ben's dad said, "We'd better head toward home." Light rain started to fall. "Faster, son," he said. The rain began coming down harder. Ben and his dad were getting soaked. Then a blue van came around the corner. "Mom!" Ben called out.

3. Koko was a gorilla. Penny, her owner, had taught the ape sign language. One day Penny asked Koko what she wanted for her birthday. "Cat," Koko answered. Penny bought a toy cat for Koko. But when Koko opened her present, she threw it down. Koko had wanted a real cat. A few months later, Penny gave Koko a real cat. Then Koko was happy.

4. Dean's grandmother was in the hospital. Dean and his mom had planned to visit her on Saturday afternoon. On Friday a friend called Dean. He asked if Dean would like to go skating Saturday afternoon. Dean loved to skate. But he told his friend that he would go skating some other time.

5. The summer night was warm and peaceful. Zack and his dad lay in their sleeping bags. They stared up at the sky together. The stars were bright. An owl hooted not far away. After a while Zack turned on his side. He went to sleep thinking about the great day it had been.

Fact	Inference	
○	○	**1.** **A.** A Venus's-flytrap is a plant.
○	○	**B.** The Venus's-flytrap's leaves snap shut.
○	○	**C.** The leaves trap the insect.
○	○	**D.** Venus's-flytraps eat insects.

Fact	Inference	
○	○	**2.** **A.** Ben and his dad enjoyed running together.
○	○	**B.** Ben's mom knew they were out running.
○	○	**C.** It was raining hard.
○	○	**D.** Ben was glad to see his mom.

Fact	Inference	
○	○	**3.** **A.** Penny was Koko's owner.
○	○	**B.** Koko wanted a cat for her birthday.
○	○	**C.** The real cat made Koko happy.
○	○	**D.** Koko was upset when she didn't get a cat.

Fact	Inference	
○	○	**4.** **A.** Dean cared about his grandmother.
○	○	**B.** Dean loved to skate.
○	○	**C.** A friend called Dean.
○	○	**D.** Dean's grandmother was sick.

Fact	Inference	
○	○	**5.** **A.** Zack had a great day.
○	○	**B.** Zack's dad took him camping.
○	○	**C.** The stars were bright.
○	○	**D.** Zack went to sleep.

1. Tanya and Margo had gone to the same school for five years. One day Margo noticed that Tanya looked sad. "What's the matter?" Margo asked. "Oh, I can't believe it!" Tanya said. "My dad got a new job in Boston. We're moving next month."

2. A coral reef is a strange and beautiful place. It has towers, tunnels, caves, and castles. But it is under the sea. The coral is made of shells from tiny animals. It looks like rock. Different kinds of fish swim around the reef. They make the reef look like a rainbow of color.

3. Kurt had taken piano lessons for the past year. Now it was the night of the spring program. Kurt hoped that his time would never come. But finally his teacher came to tell him he was next. Kurt walked on the stage. After a few minutes of playing, he stood up while the people clapped. He had played his song perfectly!

4. One of the first computers was called ENIAC. It was built in 1946. It could do about five thousand math problems in a second. Today's computers are much smaller and faster than the early ones.

5. Dodo birds once lived on some islands in the Indian Ocean. They were about the same size as a turkey. Dodos could not fly. They had a hooked beak, short legs, and a short neck. Dodo eggs were eaten by other animals on the islands. The last dodos died out over two hundred years ago.

Fact	Inference	
○	○	**1.** **A.** Tanya didn't want to move to Boston.
○	○	**B.** The girls had been friends for years.
○	○	**C.** Tanya looked sad.
○	○	**D.** Tanya's dad got a new job.

Fact	Inference	
○	○	**2.** **A.** Coral reefs are beautiful.
○	○	**B.** Fish swim around a coral reef.
○	○	**C.** The fish are colorful.
○	○	**D.** A coral reef is made of shells.

Fact	Inference	
○	○	**3.** **A.** Kurt was nervous before the program.
○	○	**B.** Kurt played his song perfectly.
○	○	**C.** The piano was on stage.
○	○	**D.** Kurt had taken piano lessons for a year.

Fact	Inference	
○	○	**4.** **A.** ENIAC was one of the first computers.
○	○	**B.** Computers today are smaller than ENIAC.
○	○	**C.** ENIAC was built in 1946.
○	○	**D.** Computers work faster than people do.

Fact	Inference	
○	○	**5.** **A.** A dodo was the size of a turkey.
○	○	**B.** The dodos died two hundred years ago.
○	○	**C.** A dodo was larger than a chicken.
○	○	**D.** Other animals ate dodo eggs.

Writing

Read each story. Then read the question that follows it. Write your answers on the lines below each question.

1. Thomas liked to visit his Uncle Benjamin. His uncle had a good sense of humor. He wrote many funny things on his writing pad. Uncle Benjamin also wrote questions about Thomas's parents. Thomas liked reading his uncle's jokes and questions. And from the smile on his uncle's face, Thomas thought Uncle Benjamin liked listening to Thomas's answers.

Why did Uncle Benjamin use a writing pad?

_____

_____

2. Marie tightened the straps on her gloves. More than a foot of snow had fallen. It looked as if she would have to work very hard. She should have bought a blower. But it was too late for that.

What is Marie going to do?

_____

_____

3. Finding the chest wasn't easy. The pirates had done a good job of hiding it. The lock on the chest was old and rusty. Opening it would be easy.

What is inside the chest?

_____

_____

To check your answers, turn to page 60.

Read the paragraph below. Then answer the questions.

The bus was almost empty when Harry got on. He sat in the back by a window. From there, he could look for signs in stores. Storeowners often put signs in their windows when they wanted help. And many storeowners might be needing part-time help in November. After a little while, the bus was crowded with people. Some were other students. Others seemed to have been out shopping. Harry wondered if he would see the right sign in a window. If he did, he'd get off the bus. But he wasn't sure he'd see any sign. Maybe there was a better way.

1. Why was Harry looking for signs?

_____

_____

2. Why did stores need part-time help in November?

_____

_____

3. What kind of person is Harry?

_____

_____

4. How old is Harry?

_____

_____

To check your answers, turn to page 60.

Check Yourself

Practice Making Inferences, Page 3
2. C

More Practice Making Inferences, Page 4
2. A. F   B. F   C. I   D. F

To check your answers to pages 6–29, see page 61.

Writing, Page 30
Possible answers include:
1. Karen kept the pot on a shelf next to a window.
2. Leon's pencil needed sharpening.
3. The dog was a guide dog or Seeing Eye dog.

Writing, Page 31
Possible answers include:
1. She thought she wasn't tall enough. She didn't think she played well enough.
2. He needs to be able to catch passes.
3. Mary is willing to learn, hard-working, and serious.
4. Mary is not certain about her skills. She seems to think she has more to learn.

To check your answers to pages 32–57, see page 62.

Writing, Page 58
Possible answers include:
1. Uncle Benjamin can't speak.
2. Marie is going to shovel snow.
3. The chest holds some kind of pirate treasure.

Writing, Page 59
Possible answers include:
1. Harry needed to find a job.
2. Holidays were coming up.
3. Harry is serious, puzzled, willing, and unsure.
4. Harry is old enough to be hired for a part-time job.

Steck-Vaughn • Comprehension Skills Series

Check Yourself

Unit 1 pp. 6–7	Unit 2 pp. 8–9	Unit 3 pp. 10–11	Unit 4 pp. 12–13	Unit 5 pp. 14–15	Unit 6 pp. 16–17	Unit 7 pp. 18–19	Unit 8 pp. 20–21	Unit 9 pp. 22–23	Unit 10 pp. 24–25	Unit 11 pp. 26–27	Unit 12 pp. 28–29
1. A	1. C	1. A	1. B	1. A	1. C	1. A	1. B	1. C	1. B	1. A	1. B
2. C	2. A	2. B	2. A	2. C	2. B	2. B	2. D	2. A	2. A	2. D	2. C
3. B	3. B	3. A	3. C	3. D	3. D	3. D	3. D	3. D	3. D	3. C	3. A
4. D	4. B	4. D	4. D	4. D	4. A	4. C	4. A	4. B	4. C	4. C	4. B
5. B	5. D	5. C	5. C	5. B	5. B	5. A	5. C	5. A	5. A	5. B	5. D

	Unit 13 pp. 32–33	Unit 14 pp. 34–35	Unit 15 pp. 36–37	Unit 16 pp. 38–39	Unit 17 pp. 40–41	Unit 18 pp. 42–43	Unit 19 pp. 44–45	Unit 20 pp. 46–47	Unit 21 pp. 48–49	Unit 22 pp. 50–51	Unit 23 pp. 52–53	Unit 24 pp. 54–55	Unit 25 pp. 56–57
1. A.	F	I	F	I	I	F	I	F	I	F	F	F	I
B.	I	F	I	F	I	I	F	F	I	I	I	F	I
C.	I	F	F	F	I	F	F	I	I	F	I	F	F
D.	F	I	I	I	I	F	I	F	F	I	F	F	F
2. A.	F	I	F	I	F	F	F	F	I	I	I	I	F
B.	F	I	I	F	F	F	I	I	F	I	F	I	F
C.	I	I	F	F	I	F	I	F	F	F	C.F	F	I
D.	F	F	I	I	I	I	F	F	F	F	I	I	F
3. A.	I	I	F	F	I	F	F	I	F	F	F	F	I
B.	F	F	I	I	I	I	I	F	I	I	F	F	F
C.	F	I	I	I	I	F	F	I	F	F	I	F	I
D.	I	F	F	F	F	F	I	F	I	I	I	I	F
4. A.	F	F	I	I	F	F	F	I	I	I	I	I	F
B.	I	I	F	I	F	F	F	F	F	I	F	F	F
C.	F	I	I	F	F	I	I	I	I	I	I	F	F
D.	F	F	F	I	I	F	F	F	F	F	F	I	I
5. A.	F	F	I	I	F	I	I	I	F	F	F	F	F
B.	I	F	I	F	I	I	I	F	F	I	I	I	F
C.	F	F	I	I	I	F	F	F	I	F	F	F	I
D.	I	I	F	F	F	I	F	F	F	I	I	F	F